We Read!

Dr. Carol Thompson

Topaz Publishing

READING ENTERTAINMENT FOR THE ENTIRE FAMILY

Copyright© November, 2013, Dr. Carol Thompson

Cover Art: Dawne Dominque Copyright November 2013

Editor: Arianna Alexander, Topaz Publishing

Line Editor: Topaz Publishing

Genre: Juvenile

Topaz Line: Topaz Jr.

ISBN: TPEB000000043

ISBN-13: 978-0615930282 (Topaz Publishing)

ISBN-10: 061593028X

TOPAZ PUBLISHING, LLC

USA

www.topazpublishingllc.com

Topaz Publishing, LLC

DEDICATION

We Read!

By: Dr. Carol Thompson

Dedicated to: every single student at VanWert Elementary School in Rockmart, GA. You make my job fun! Hugs & Books!

Special Dedication to: Zach Thompson, my big baby boy who helped me put these words together. I love you.

Morgan Thompson, always my "sweet pea". I love you.

Dear Parent, Guardian, Caregiver, Educator, or Friend,

I will not bore you with the multitude of research that says reading is important. Just know that I have studied and researched this topic endlessly. In a nutshell, reading increases vocabulary, raises test scores, and promotes social, emotional, and intellectual growth. It is the means to every end. My dissertation was entitled "Bibliotherapy and Anxiety". Bibliotherapy is a long word that only means "Reading helps heal". My strongest desire is to instill the love of reading in every child my voice or pen touches.

With love in my heart and a book in my hand, I challenge you to read with your child. Model not only the skill of reading, but also the LOVE of reading. Like my friends in this book, I hope you will find a unique and creative place to read.

"Hugs and Books!"

Dr. Carol Thompson ♥

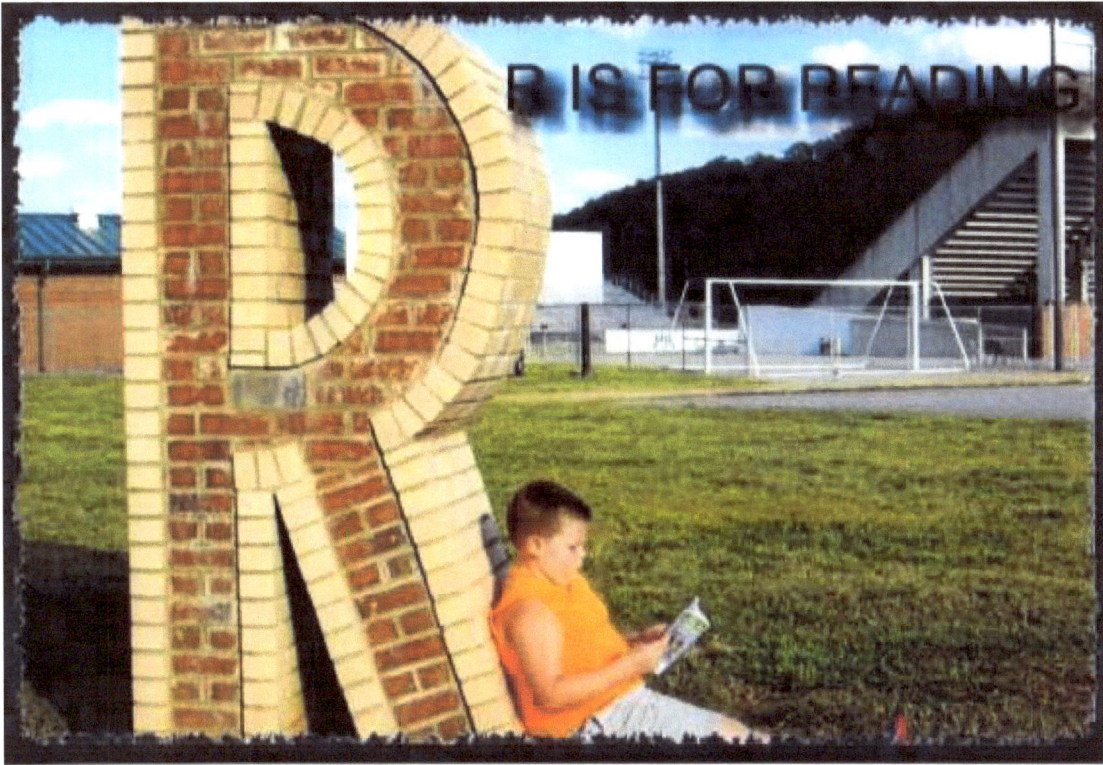

Reading is FUN! Reading is COOL!

We read lots of places, and not just at SCHOOL!

We read to our pets, and we read quite a lot,

To our kittens, our pigs, or even to Spot.

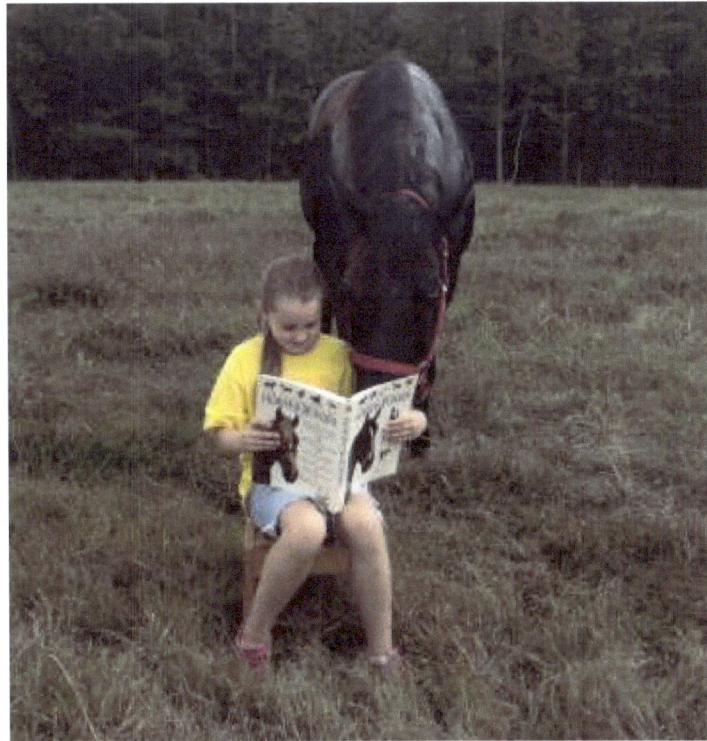

We read to our horses. We read to ourselves.

We pick great books right off of the shelves!

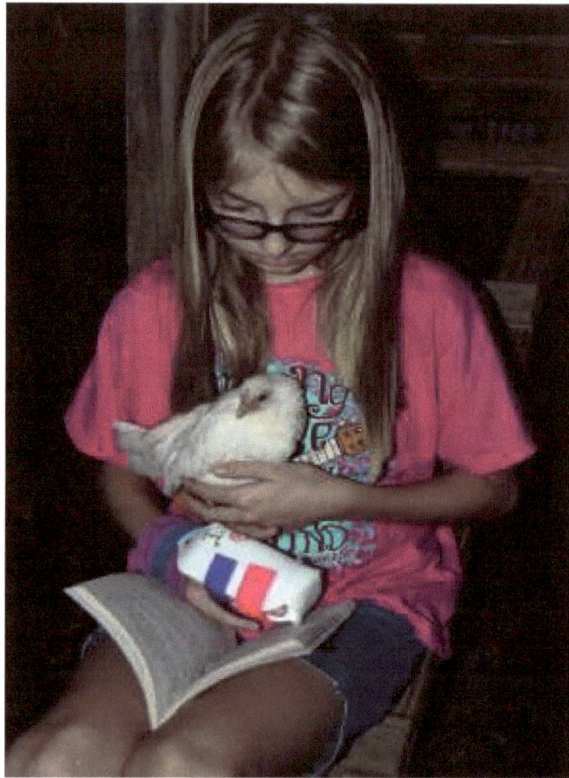

We read to our roosters. We read to our hens.

We read while sitting on top of their pens.

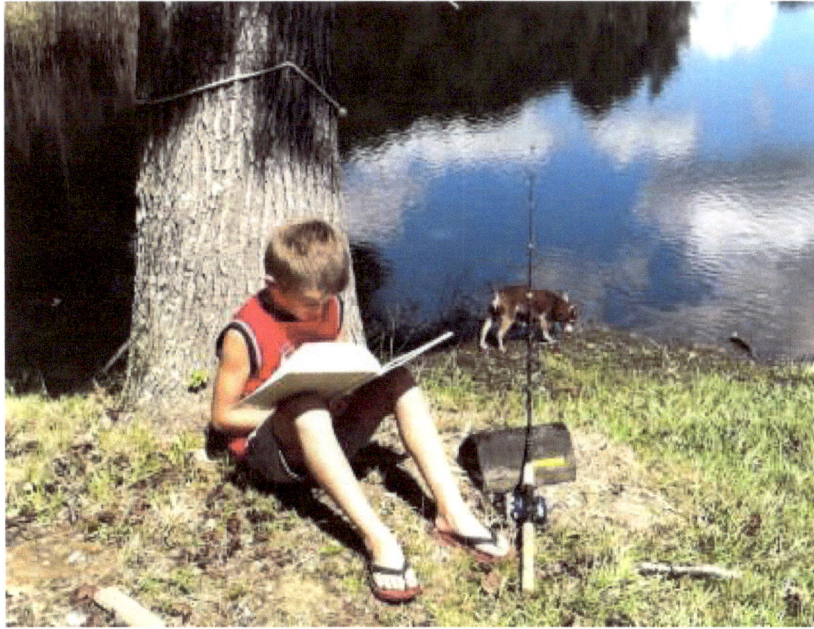

We read in quiet and peaceful locations.

Sometimes, we read while we're on vacation.

We read far out, and deep in the country.

Sometimes, we're home and read with our family.

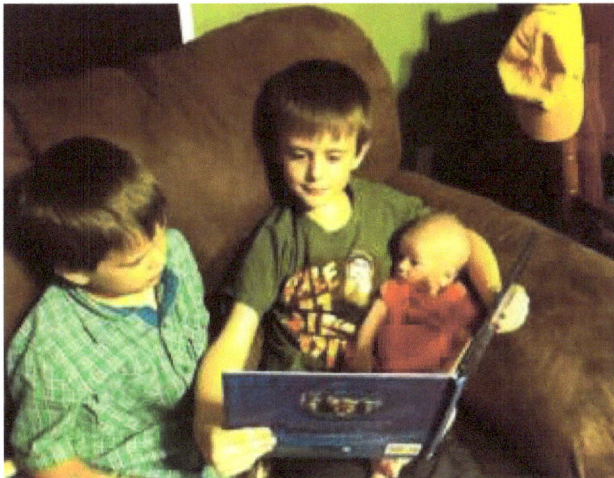

We read to our sisters, and read to our brothers.

We read with our fathers, but mostly our mothers.

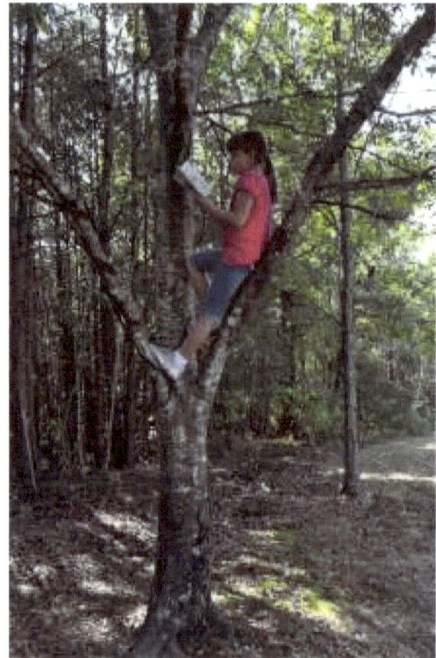

We read in high, and way up places,

And sometimes we read in very tight spaces.

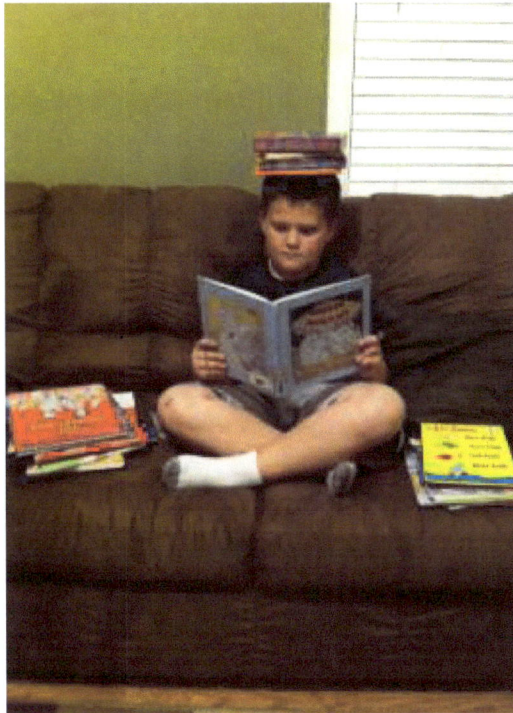

Sometimes we read with books on our heads,

Or perched in a tree, and quiet instead.

We frequently read while playing our sports;

The football field, gym, or basketball courts.

Reading all fancy in ribbons and bows,

Reading while dancing and pointing our toes!

Ballerinas read while wearing their tutus!

Books, books, books, we sure love you!

We read on our picnic; our basket can wait.

We will read for St. Nick, if he isn't too late.

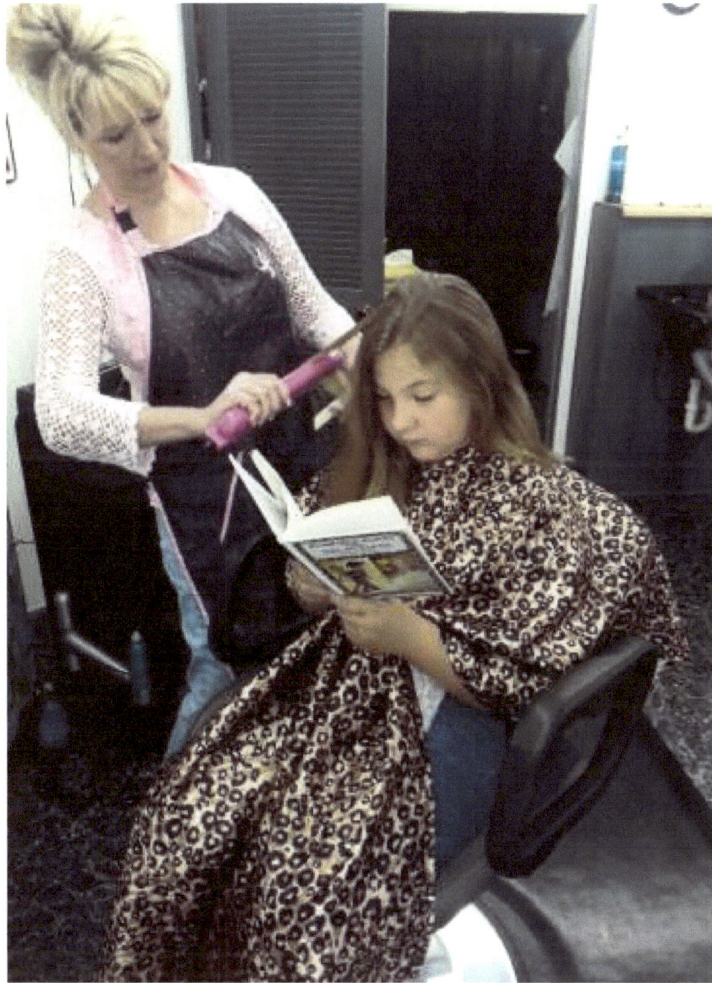

We read and get pretty at the beauty salon.

We read on the rooftops while sitting alone.

We love to read hanging upside down.

We read our books all over the town.

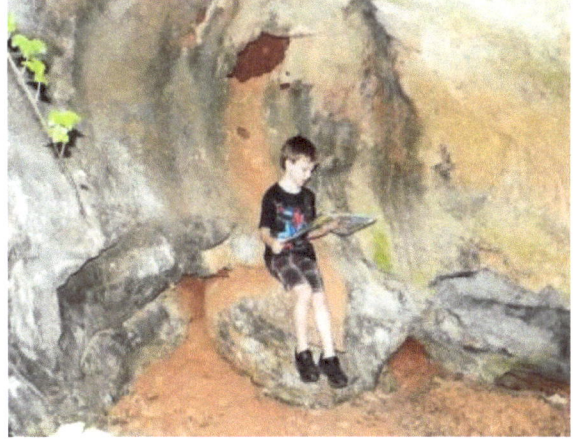

We read eerie stories inside of caves.

We read spooky books in front of old graves.

We read while we're waiting, and on the go.

The more you read, the more you will know!

We read in the sun when we go out to play.

We even read on our special birthday!

We read in the country— down on the farm.

We read on the tractor, or inside the barn.

We read while checking out things on the ranch.

We read and lounge on a strong tree branch.

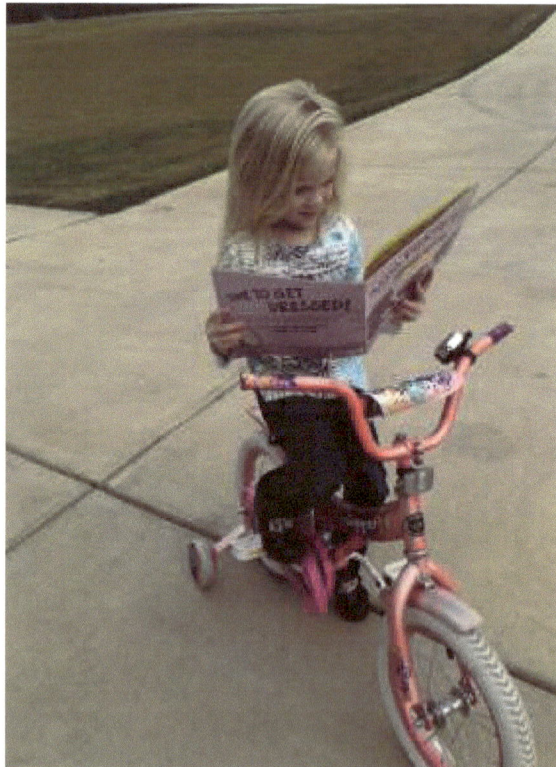

We read sometimes while riding a bike.

There's not one book we did not like.

We read while playing make believe.

Books are the best gift you'll ever receive.

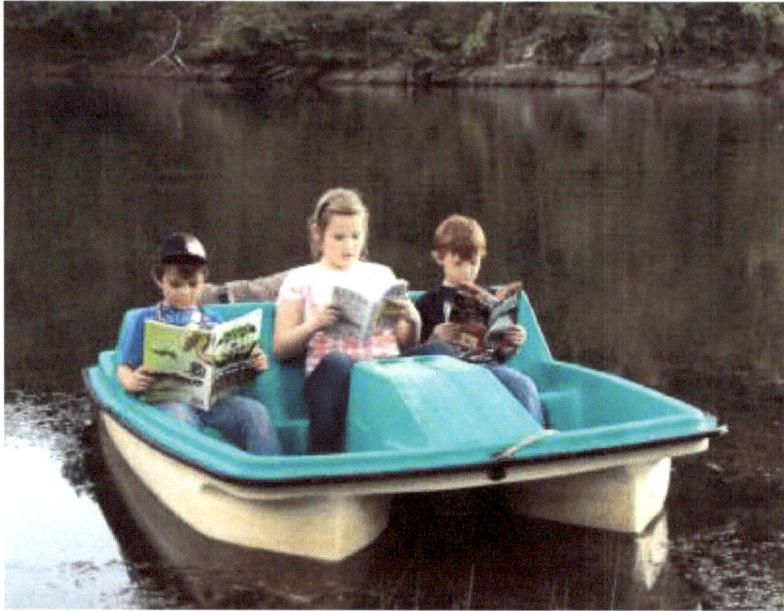

We read at the lake and in our boat.

Stories come to life when we are afloat.

We read our books on the busy playground.

Books, books, books, they're all around.

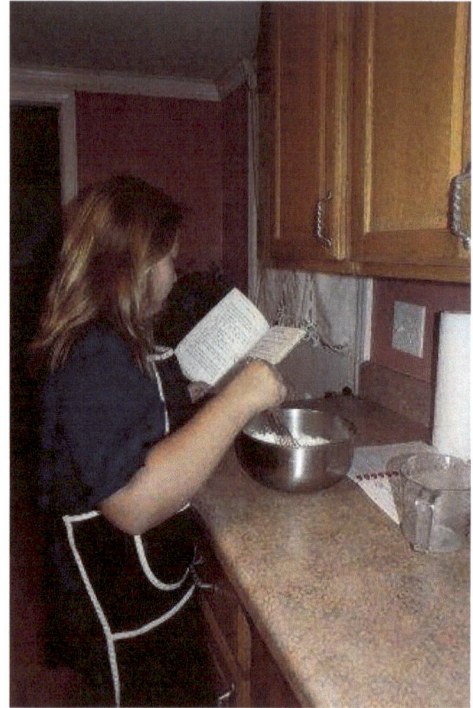

We read while jumping so high in the sky.

We read while making a chocolate pie.

We read on top of many things.

We even read on front porch swings.

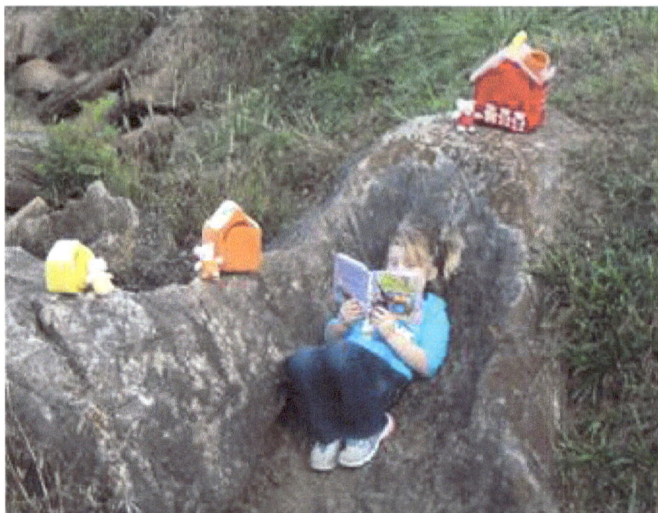

We read while lying on really big rocks.

We read with bare feet and no tight socks.

We read on the mailbox. We read inside pens.

We read good books, again and again.

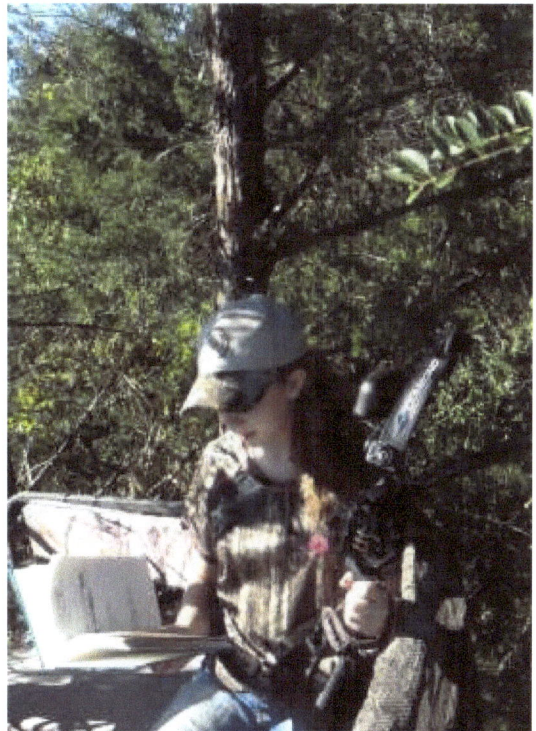

READING IS GOOD!
1. Higher Test Scores
2. Increase Vocabulary
3. Social Growth
4. Intellectual Growth

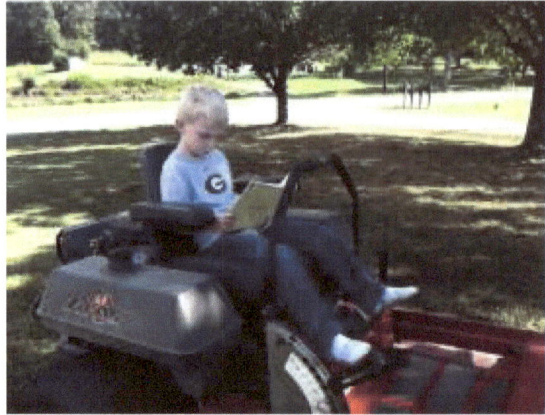

We read while sitting on awesome machines.

Make reading a part of your daily routine.

We read in dump trucks, and bulldozers too.

We read in the cornfield when our work is all through.

We read at the store in our very own carts,

Or at the garage, inside of our cars!

We read while we're walking.

We read while we run.

We read and read 'till the book is all done.

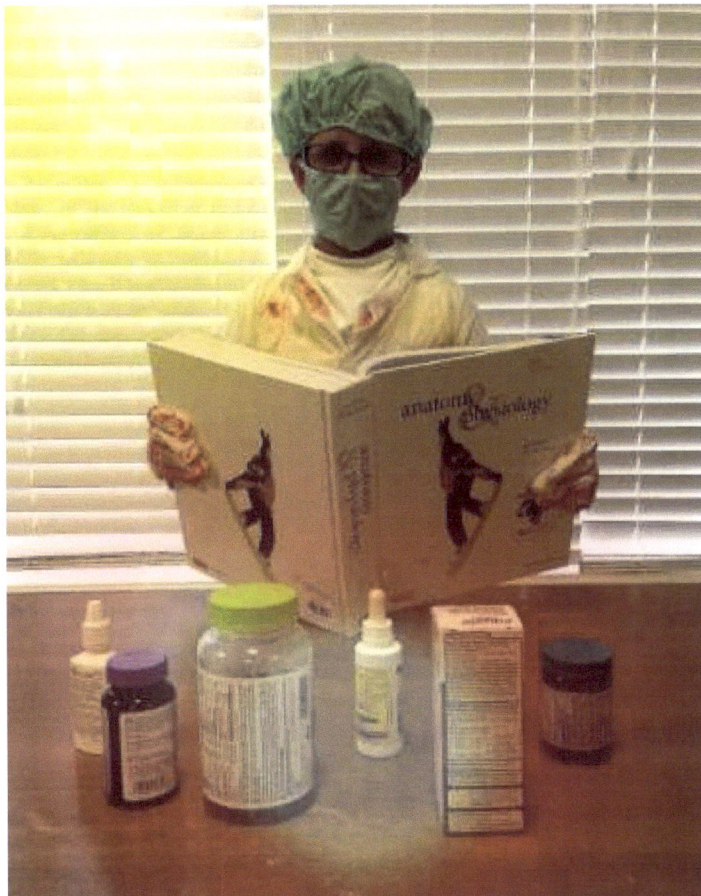

We read while dressed-up and playing pretend.

Sometimes, we just like to read with a friend.

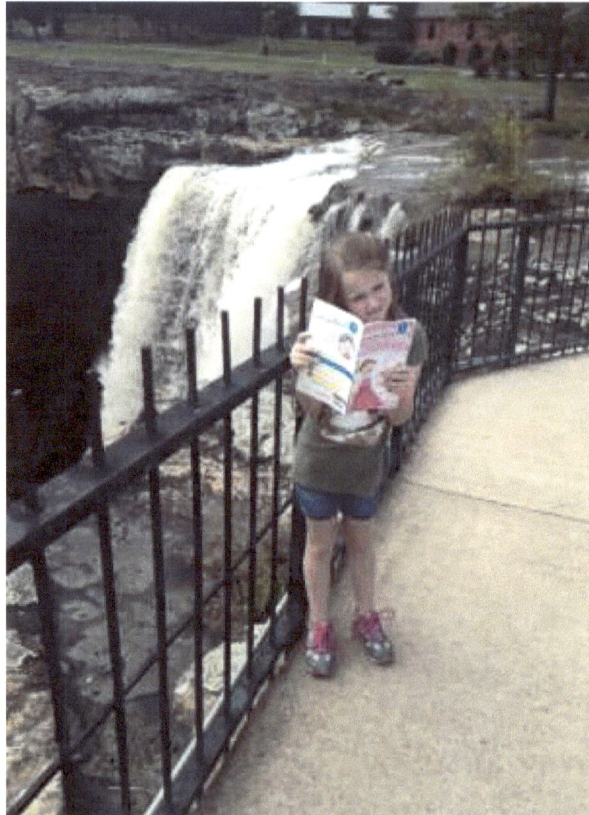

We read in front of noisy waterfalls.

At times, we read softly while playing with dolls.

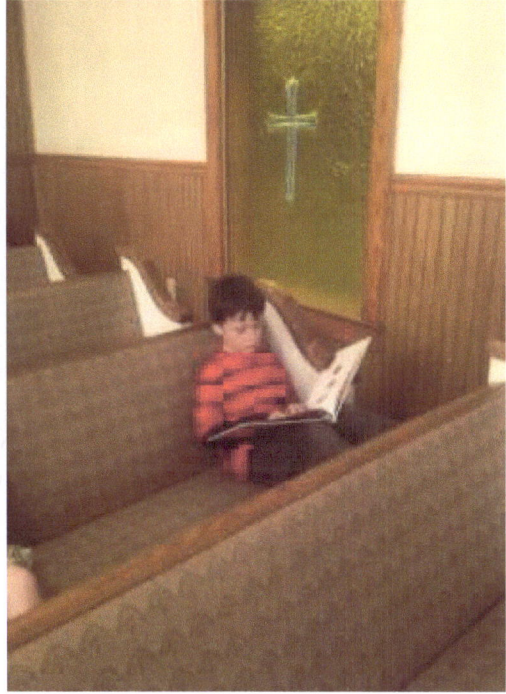

We can read in church,

Or read at the mall.

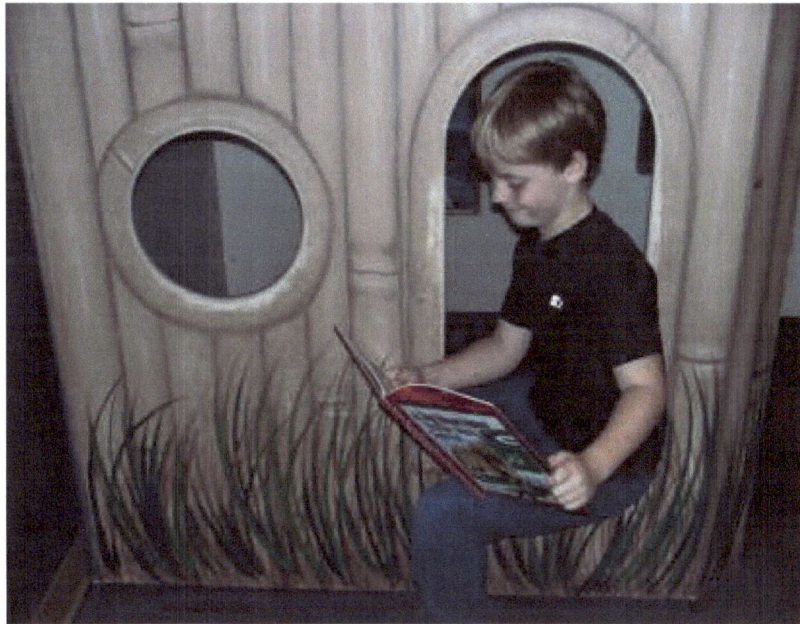

We read books, books, books, 'till we've read them all.

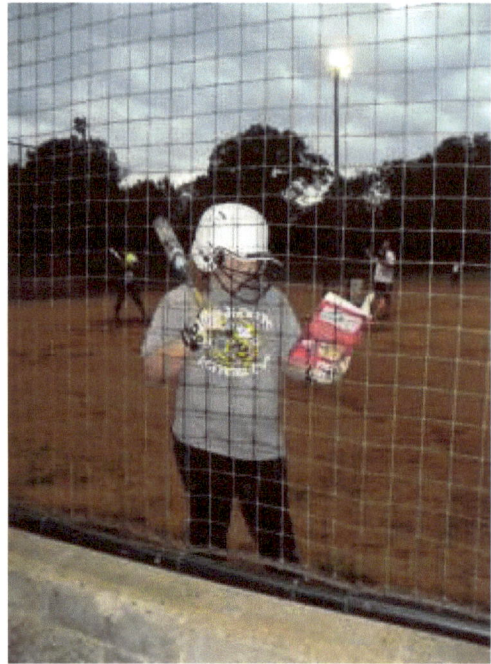

There are hundreds of places where we like to read,

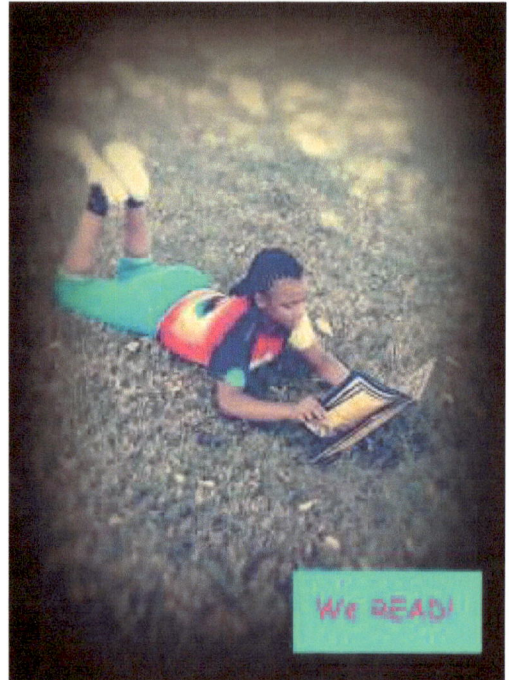

Unique and creative, GUARANTEED!

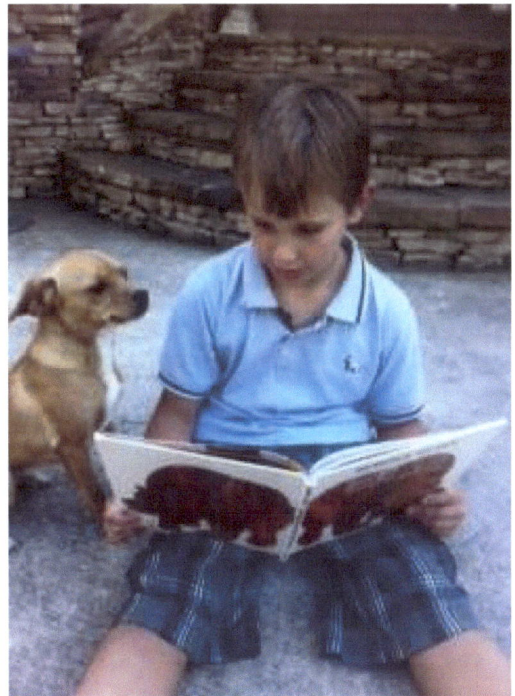

Where will you read, if given the time?

You pick your spot, and I will pick mine!

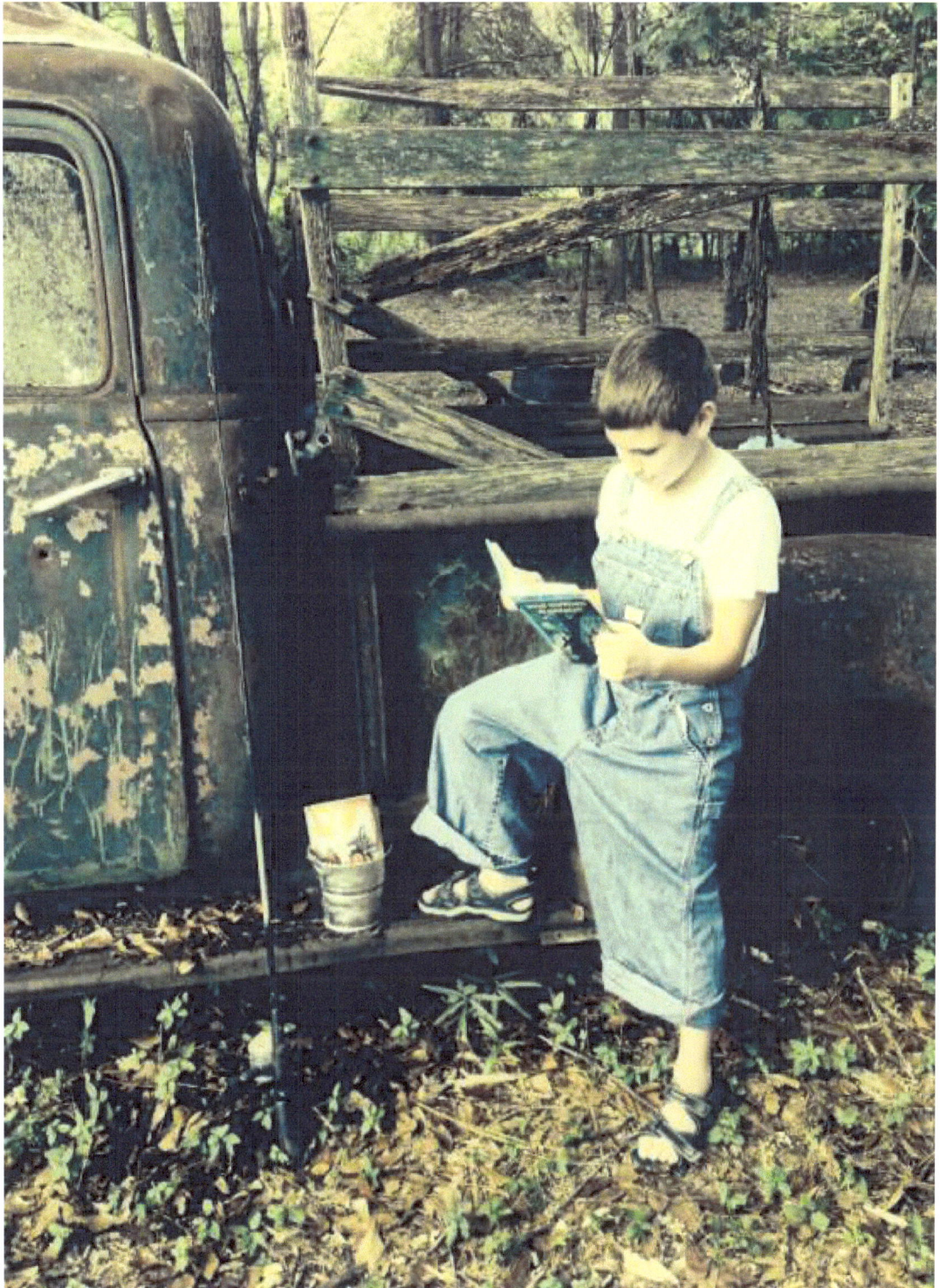

BOOKS ARE A TIMELESS TREASURE.

WHERE IS YOUR FAVORITE PLACE TO READ?

PASTE YOUR PICTURE HERE

THIS IS MY FAVORITE PLACE TO READ!

About the Author.

Dr. Carol Thompson

Dr. Thompson is a media specialist at Van Wert Elementary School. She understands the value of literacy and tries all sorts of ways to get her students to read. Carol has authored several books and countless magazine articles. In her spare time she loves to travel with her family and scrapbook the memories they make. She lives in Rockmart, GA, with her husband, son, daughter, and one very spoiled Schnauzer.

Learn More About Dr. Carol Thompson

Cdthomp@bellsouth.net

http://cdthomp.wix.com/carolthompson

https://www.facebook.com/carol.thompsonauthor.9

http://www.topazpublishingllc.com